Secrets of Success for Women

the
Home

KAREN H WHITING

LIVING
INK
BOOKS
Writing Worth Reading

AMG Publishers
6815 Shallowford Road
Chattanooga
Tenessee 37421

Designed by
ANDREW MILNE DESIGN

ISBN 0-89957-123-9

Printed by South China Printing Company,
China

CONTENTS

God and home

All plans and building a life as a family hold the promise of success when God is the builder.

*Unless the LORD builds the **house**, its builders labor in vain. Psalm 127:1a*

God desires a love relationship with every family. His advice is to love him and include him in all the little moments of family life.

Hear, O Israel: The LORD our God, the LORD is one. Love the LORD your God with all your heart and with all your soul and with all your strength. These commandments that I give you today are to be upon your hearts. Impress them on your children. Talk about them when you sit at home and when you walk along the road, when you lie down and when you get up. Deuteronomy 6:4-7

Invite God into home life from rising to bedtime, and from casual times while eating to physical activities.

Tie them as symbols on your hands and bind them on your foreheads. Write them on the doorframes of your houses and on your gates. Deuteronomy 6:8-9

God also desires that we weave his presence into the fabric of daily life by adorning ourselves and decorating our homes with symbols that remind us of him.

ADORNMENT TIPS

- Hang a special doorknocker on your door, such as a fish or cross.
- For holidays add door decorations that use Christian symbols.
- Wear a cross, rainbow, or other Christian jewelry.
- Light a candle at meals as a reminder of the presence of the one creator of light!
- Keep a Bible out and read from it daily, as though reading a love letter.
- Hang a Christian picture or verse above each bed.
- Use a nightlight in a child's room as a reminder that God keeps watch at all times.

MOMS PARTNERED WITH GOD

How many make a family? It only takes two and God promises to be one of the two or more.

A father to the fatherless, a defender of widows, is God in his holy dwelling. Psalm 68:5

God promises to be father to the fatherless and a partner to widows. If there is no man at home consider yourself not a single mom or single person, but a parent or woman partnered with God.

Christ and home

Jesus replied, "If anyone loves me, he will obey my teaching. My Father will love him, and we will come to him and make our **home** *with him." John* 14:23

> "Christ is the Head of this House
> The unseen Guest at every meal
> The silent listener to every conversation."
>
> Author unknown

DESIRES OF WOMEN WHO SEEK CHRIST'S PRESENCE IN THE HOME

- Love permeates relationships
- Peace reigns
- Children grow up knowing Christ as Savior
- Love that spills over into ministry
- An atmosphere where family loves to stay and others love to visit
- Jesus enjoyed and cared about families. He attended weddings, meals, and God's plan for marriage. John 2:1-10; Matthew 8:14-15, 19:6, 14; Mark 8:1-9, and Luke 7:11-15

KEEPING CHRIST'S PRESENCE AT HOME WITH DAILY ACTIONS

- Devote yourself to God's Word and living it.
- Set a plate with bread at meals as a sign of the presence of Christ, the bread of life.
- Hug family members and say, "Jesus loves you!"
- Read and discuss one Bible verse at each meal.
- Schedule quiet time for yourself to refill your heart with God's love.

Mary and Joseph's example shows us important goals
of a PARENT

Prioritize by placing your child's well-being first.
*So he [Joseph] got up, took the child and his mother during
the night and left for Egypt. Matthew 2:14*
Joseph acted immediately when an angel urged him
to flee to Egypt to protect Jesus.

Always be a supportive Anchor and
Advocate for your child, even during their
trials. *Near the cross of Jesus stood his mother, his
mother's sister.... John 19:25a*

Raise a child to be Responsible and trust a
grown child to do the right things. *His mother said
to the servants, "Do whatever he tells you." John 2:5*

Exercise authority. *Then he went down
to Nazareth with them and was obedient to them
[his parents]. Luke 2:51a*

Nurture a child to grow in mental, physical,
relational, and spiritual areas.
*And Jesus grew in wisdom and stature, and in favor with
God and men. Luke 2:52*

Treasure the uniqueness of each child.
*But his mother treasured all these things in her heart.
Luke 2:51b*
Mary did not understand others' comments about
Jesus or her son's words and actions, but she
cherished them.

Spouse and teamwork

Greet Priscilla and Aquila, my fellow workers in Christ Jesus. They risked their lives for me. Not only I but all the churches of the gentiles are grateful to them. Romans 16:3-4

TEAMwork

Priscilla and her husband, Aquila, formed a team. Together they opened their home to Paul and lovingly reached out to the church community. Their story is in Acts 18.

Elements of teamwork for spouses
Time spent together develops a relationship.
Education in Scriptures keeps a godly focus.
Actions based on faith make life fruitful and rich.
Ministry together keeps God in the center of the relationship.

Couples may not share all interests and activities but should support and respect one another's choices.

PARENTING AS A TEAM

Ephesians 5:22-33 paints a picture of the relation between husband and wife as that of Christ and the church. The passage directs a wife to submit to her husband and to respect him. Submit is to yield. Respect means to honor or hold someone in high regard.

Tips for wives

- Trust your spouse.
- Trust your spouse's decisions.
- Forgive your spouse for any and all hurts.
- Safeguard intimacy and shortcomings.
- Praise your spouse's talents, actions, and virtues.
- Listen with your eyes, ears, and heart.
- Serve your husband joyfully as Christ served others.
- Consider your spouse's needs, efforts, and emotions.

Studies continually show that the most well adjusted children come from homes with both parents still married. Whether focusing on discipline, training, play, or rewards, talk and choose together how to raise your children.

SPOUSE HONORING SPOUSE

It works best when a parent corrects children to honor the opposite spouse. An easy reminder is, "I love your dad. It hurts to hear you talk back to him. Say that you are sorry."

MOMS PARTNERED WITH GOD

Remind your children that God their father loves you and it hurts him to hear unkind words about someone he loves.

> "If there is not that obedience and surrender **of the father and mother to each other,** there can be very little courage in the parents to ask that obedience of their children. And if today we are having all the troubles with family life, I think it began there."
>
> *Mother Teresa*

Modeling Christ in marriage

LOVE ATTRIBUTE	APPLICATIONS IN MARRIAGE
Patient	Listen attentively Work slowly at changes Gently remind spouse of problems
Kind	Do little tasks to please spouse Praise spouse with words
Humility	Willingly admit wrong and ask for forgiveness
Not proud	Willingly forgive hurts Listen and accept spouse's constructive criticism
Polite/Not rude	Say please and thank you to spouse Disagree gently and with clearly stated reasons
Other focused/ Not self-seeking	Consider spouse's feelings/desires first Cook, clean, and care for home to please family Work at building a home that is loving and open
Not angered easily	When hurt, stop, pray, and think of spouse's feelings Learn to have an attitude of gratitude

Your attitude should be the same as that of Christ Jesus.
Philippians 2:5

As two become one, the partnership serves as a single
witness to their children and the world.
In a love relationship, pattern your actions on the
great chapter on love, 1 Corinthians 13:4-11.

No counting wrongs	Forget past hurts, forgive, and don't bring them up again Remember and treasure acts of love
Rejoices in truth	Share honestly with spouse Understand problems are God's way of disciplining
Protects	Keep the marriage bed sacred Do not gossip about spouse's habits/actions
Trusts	Be trustworthy Believe in spouse's words
Hopes	Share future dreams with spouse Keep trusting God's plans
Perseveres	During hard times, work hard, wait on God Support spouse's choices Help find solutions to problems
Never fails	Never give up, even in hard times Always remember love is a commitment
Not childish	Do not belittle spouse, or play games for attention Do not spend money foolishly or independently

Church family & support

Yet to all who received him, to those who believed in his name, he gave the right to become children of God. John 1:12

Jesus invites everyone to be part of the larger family of God. This makes the church an extended family for everyone to find and give support.

EXAMPLES OF MINISTRIES THAT SUPPORT FAMILIES

- Children's church
- Children's education
- Youth groups
- MOPS groups
- Adult Bible studies
- Homemaker groups
- Babysitting co-ops
- Prayer groups
- Sport groups
- Marriage enrichment groups
- Hardhat groups to help singles with repairs
- Financial support groups to help people manage money/become debt free

SERVICE OPPORTUNITIES FOR FAMILIES
> Feeding and clothing homeless
> Missions
> Nursing home visitation groups
> Help in the ministries that support family
> Pray for pastors, church workers, and church
> ministries

ß

PRO-ACTIVE FAMILIES
All the believers were together and had everything in common.
Acts 2:44

Choose to be in fellowship with your church
community. Make friends there. Study the Bible with
others. Share yourself and your resources within
your church community.

CHURCH FELLOWSHIP OPPORTUNITIES
- Check out the groups at your church.
- Start a new group that may be needed.
- Build friendships with people at church.
- Greet people at church.
- Attend social gatherings
  at church.

ß

Therefore, as we have opportunity,
let us do good to all people, especially
to those who belong to the **family** *of*
believers. Galatians 6:10

Blessing the home

"But if serving the LORD seems undesirable to you, then choose for yourselves this day whom you will serve, whether the gods your forefathers served beyond the River, or the gods of the Amorites, in whose land you are living. But as for me and my **household**, we will serve the LORD." Joshua 24:15

The choice to serve the Lord is up to each family. Choose to serve and ask for Christ's blessing upon your household. Household includes the members of the family, workers in the home, and the building. You may also ask God to bless your cars and other possessions.

WHY A BLESSING?

Blessing a home reminds people that God is in control. It shows we trust God to care for our family and property. It is also a commitment to choose to serve Christ and use possessions for Christian service. It helps children see their house as a place of refuge from the world. A prayer of blessing invites Christ to be present in the home and daily life of the family.

SCRIPTURE BLESSING

Now be pleased to bless the house of your servant, that it may continue forever in your sight; for you, O Sovereign LORD, have spoken, and with your blessing the house of your servant will be blessed forever. 2 Samuel 7:29

Other verses to read or pray
Proverbs 24:3-4
Matthew 7:24-27

IRISH HOUSE BLESSING

Bless this house, O Lord, we pray. Make it safe by night and day. Bless these walls so firm and stout, keeping want and trouble out. Bless the roof and chimney tall, let thy peace lie over all. Bless the doors that they may prove, ever open to joy and love. Bless the windows shining bright, letting in God's heavenly light. Bless the hearth a-blazing there, with smoke ascending like a prayer. Bless the people here within; keep them pure and free from sin. Bless us all, that one day, we may be fit, O Lord, to dwell with Thee.

VISUAL REMINDERS

In the movie, *It's a Wonderful life*, the Baileys used three symbols while blessing their home:
Bread ("that this house will never know hunger")
Salt ("that life will always have flavor")
Wine ("that joy and prosperity will reign forever")

Other people light a candle upon entering each room and praying for Christ to fill it with his light and love.

Prayer habits

Be joyful in hope, patient in affliction, faithful in prayer.
Romans 12:12

Prayer is our link to Jesus. Better than wireless phones
or the Internet, the connection is always strong and
never breaks down. Scriptures remind us to be
faithful in prayer and continuously pray, even when
we do not receive immediate answers. Each person
should develop a habit of praying daily and the
family should also spend time together in prayer.

SIMPLE WAYS TO PRAY AS A FAMILY

Blessings of parents
Lay your hand on each child and ask Christ to bless
your child.

Echo prayers
Use a line of Scripture or a simple phrase and let
everyone echo that between people praying. You
may want a theme for this, such as a prayer time of
thanksgiving. For example, after each person thanks
Jesus for something, everyone echoes, "Thank you,
Lord, for all you give us."

Scripture prayers
Let each person read a portion of a Psalm or other
Bible passage.

POW-WOW

Ask each person to state one POW or worry, and one WOW, something for which they are thankful. Have the next person say a simple Prayer Over the Worry and a little praise or Worship Over the WOW. Then that person gives a POW and a WOW.

Dish up prayers

Set out four bowls. In one, place words for God (Creator, Lord, Jesus); in one, place words for people (child, sinner); in another, place prayer verbs (thanks, asks, praises); and in the last, place words for objects of prayer (healing, money, friendship, problem). Take turns drawing out a word from each container and putting them together to form a prayer. (Creator, child, thanks, and friendship may become, "Creator, your child thanks you for your friendship.")

TIMES TO PRAY AS A FAMILY

Before school

Before meals

Before bed

When a problem arises

After receiving gifts

Before trips

When someone is hurt or sad

Before and after sporting events or other activities

ß'

The Lord's Prayer

"This, then, is how you should pray: 'Our Father in heaven, hallowed be your name.' "

Matthew 6:9

Jesus gave us a model for prayer when his disciples asked him how to pray. Celebrate this prayer Jesus gave us with a ceremony and learn from the words. Use 11 candles. Make a paper symbol for each and pin it on. As you light each candle, say the prayer phrase and then talk about the meaning.

PRAYER PHRASE	SYMBOL	MEANING
Our Father	Number one in white	This is a greeting. There is only one God and he is pure and holy.
In heaven	Clouds with two eyes	God in heaven always watches over us.
Hallowed be your name	Green tree	This is a praise. The evergreen tree is a symbol of an ever-Holy God.
Your kingdom come	Purple crown	Purple is the color for royalty The crown symbolizes a king.
Your will be done on earth as it is in heaven	One-way sign on a brown path.	We know God's plans are best We agree on earth to choose the one way to follow God's will.
Give us today our daily bread	Yellow loaf of bread.	Prayer is also time to ask for help Bread is a symbol for Jesus, the bread of life. We ask for both physical and spiritual food.
Forgive us our debts, as we also have forgiven our debtors	Silver coin	A coin is a symbol for paying a debt. We ask for forgiveness if we hurt someone. We also agree to forgive anyone who has hurt us.
And lead us not into temptation	Black square	Have nothing to do with the darkness of sin. Ask for help with any bad habits.
But deliver us from the evil one	Cross made of 5 red hearts	Jesus loved us enough to give his life to save us. Trust Jesus for safety from evil.
For yours is the kingdom and the power	Gold treasure box with red hearts in it	God's real treasure is our hearts We have hope because God is in charge.
And the glory forever	Orange flame	An orange flame is for God who is light. We want to give God glory.
Amen		Amen means we agree.

Family devotions

Therefore everyone who hears these words of mine and puts them into practice is like a wise man who built his **house** *on the rock. Matthew 7:24*

Devoted means to be loyal and faithful.
  A family devotion is a time to build faith
  and loyalty while gathering together.

A devotion can be reading one verse and discussing it,
  or it can be a fun activity, such as a game, in which a
  Scripture is read and discussed then linked to the
  activity, such as talking about spiritual perseverance
  after playing a game.

PACK Devotions For Success
  Make devotions so much fun that your family
  clamors to do them!
  Praise your children for showing the value seen
  in the devotion. If you read about someone being
  generous praise your child's generous actions.
  Children love to be caught doing good and to feel
  their parents' approval.
  Add Applications to use. Share ideas on how each
  person can apply the lesson starting right away.
  For example, a lesson about Cain can lead to
  applications on anger management. Application
  makes the Bible relevant.

Celebrate success after completing devotions.
Save dessert or other fun for after devotions and use
it as an incentive, too. If there's no time for God's
sweet Word then there's no time for sweet treats.
This extends the together time with fun like adding
a cherry and whipped cream that turns ice cream
into a sundae.

Keep devotion time short. When you cannot finish
a planned reading or activity within your time limit,
save the rest for the next time. Aim for 10-20 minutes.

TRY VARIETY

- Do a science experiment and connect it to
  Bible truths, such as sowing seeds after reading the
  parable of the sower.
- Act out a Bible passage.
- Watch a Christian video, discuss it, and relate it to
  a Bible verse.
- Sing Christian music and talk about the words.
- Cook a food talked about in the Bible.
- Try a Bible sport like archery (*1 Samuel* 20:18-40)
  or running (*1 Corinthians* 9:24-27) and discuss the
  Bible stories involving the sport.
- Make Scriptures visual by showing objects in the
  Bible passage such as lighting a candle when
  reading about being a light in Matthew 5:14.
- Have a mother-daughter, father-son, or other
  parent-child devotion.

13'

I have been reminded of your sincere faith, which first lived in your grandmother Lois and in your mother Eunice and, I am persuaded, now lives in you also. 2 Timothy 1:5

Paul praised a young man's family for passing on their faith. Timothy's grandmother and mother modeled and shared their faith with Timothy.
We can do that with our children.

WAYS A DAD CAN STILL BE THE SPIRITUAL LEADER WHEN AWAY FROM HOME

❀ Shop online for a devotion book. Dad can inscribe the book with a note or a prayer to be said at the opening or closing of devotions.

❀ Audio/video tape devotions before leaving on trips. He can read a passage and ask questions where the tape player can be stopped for children to provide answers.

❀ Have children draw the lesson and write a summary caption to show Dad.

❀ Time phone calls for the end of devotions for Dad to join in.

❀ Buy duplicate books for Dad to read along while away.

❀ Tape devotion time so Dad can listen later.

☙

UNEXPECTED BLESSINGS

Devotionals teach children about God but also provide other unseen benefits.

- Develops cognitive skills of reading comprehension and vocabulary.
- Builds communication skills or listening, sharing, eye contact, etc.
- Children learn to converse with adults on a variety of topics.
- Provides discussion on topics from a neutral perspective (easier to talk about Peter's failure than our own, especially for a child).
- Builds memories.
- Gives children a spiritual heritage.

♌

APPLY DEVOTIONS TO LIFE

Understand that in every little situation, there's a life value or principle that can be taught or reinforced. Fights over toys provide opportunities to teach about being content, not being jealous, patience, or generosity. After a fight is settled consider what value you want to develop and think of a related devotion. Remind children of that devotion and the value (sharing, contentment, etc.).

When you continue having the same problems, that's when you need to really think about the virtue lacking and find devotions related to the problem.

RESOURCES:

Family Devotional Builder by Karen H Whiting, Hendrickson, ISBN 1-56563-567-1

Bible Discovery Devotions by Martha Larchar, Concordia Publishing House, ISBN 0570052254

Playtime Devotions by Christine Tangvald, Standard Publishing, ISBN 0784713618

Biblical models

The act of faith is what distinguished our ancestors, set them above the crowd. Hebrews 11:2 (MSG)

Study models of women with families in the Bible. Discover how family members interacted and relied on God.

GOOD EXAMPLES

1 Peter 3:5 refers to holy women of old whose gentle and quiet spirits brought praise.

❀ Eve sinned and repented. She recognized a child as a gift from God. *(Genesis 2:20–4:2; 4:17; 1 Timothy 2:13-14)*

❀ Sarah followed her husband's advice, even when it brought trouble, and laughed in her old age when she finally became a mother. *(Genesis 11:31–12:17; 21; Romans 9:9)*

❀ Ruth and Naomi became in-laws and widows who supported one another. Ruth's servant attitude and generous spirit won her a husband and special place in the lineage of Christ. She trusted God in difficult times. *(Ruth)*

❀ Deborah worked as a judge, cared for her family, and sought God's guidance. *(Judges 4–5)*

B

Paul and others praised many women in the
early church.

❀ Lois and Eunice taught Timothy as a child
to know and follow Scriptures. (*2 Timothy 1:5*)
❀ Dorcas served others with sewing and caring
for the needy. Her church family loved her.
(*Acts 9:32-42*)
❀ Priscilla served with her husband at home and
on short-term missionary trips. (*Acts 18:1-3, 26;
Romans 16:3; 2 Timothy 4:19*)
❀ Lydia opened her home to missionaries.
(*Acts 16:14-15*)

❧

BAD EXAMPLES
❀ Jezebel worshipped idols and plotted murder
out of a greedy heart. She died a violent death.
(*1 Kings 16:31-33; 18:4-13; 19:1-2; 21:1-15, 23;
2 Kings 9:7, 30-37*)
❀ Herodias used her daughter to ask the king
to kill a prophet. Her guilt over sin grew to a
hateful grudge. (*Matthew 14:3-12; Mark 6:17*)
❀ God saved Lot's daughters yet they failed to trust
the future to God and took matters into their
own hands. They committed incest and started
evil nations. (*Genesis 19:30-38*)

❧

Look for the virtues or vices of each biblical woman.
Consider how their choices should influence your
choices.

Treasuring family

Sons are a heritage from the Lord, children a reward from him. Psalm 127:3

TREASURE UNIQUENESS IN EACH PERSON

    Affirm each person's interests.

    Observe natural choices made in clothing,
food, activities, subjects, books, etc.

    Find ways to encourage talents and passions.

    Pray for each person and ask God to reveal the
treasured gifts within each one.

TREAT EACH PERSON AS A TREASURE

    Praise loved ones.

    Accept individuals as specially created by God.

    Express love and acceptance to family members.

    Forgive mistakes.

    Catch family members doing good deeds.

    Hug and kiss each loved one often.

    Be available. Let your family know each person
is a priority.

    Place something of beauty that reflects each
person's interests in his or her room.

    Remember that to a child T-I-M-E spells love.

    Follow correction with affirming your love.

GUARD THE TREASURE

    Safeguard your child. Meet and get to know
people involved with them.

Account for where your child goes and who your child spends time with.

Frequently remind them to tell you if someone tries to touch or hurt them.

Establish loving limits, sensible rules, and consequences. Enforce the rules.

TREASURE MEMORIES

Take photos and make scrapbooks of time together. Add in verses and memories of God and your loved one.

SEEK TREASURE

Look and discover gifts and talents in each person.

Ask others about your loved one to find out what qualities others notice. (Teachers, relatives, friends, co-workers)

As you uncover hidden qualities rejoice and talk about the discoveries.

FILL HEARTS WITH TREASURE SO EACH PERSON WILL CHERISH FAMILY

Heritage treasure
Share family stories and retell experiences.

Emotional treasure
Provide rich emotional experiences

Affectionate treasure
Use positive and loving words and physical touch

Relational treasure
Spend time together and interact

Team treasure
Involve everyone in choices and participation

Scripture treasure
Weave God's Word into family life

"For where your treasure is, there your heart will be also."
Matthew 6:21

Servant love

Then they (older women) can train the younger women to love their husbands and children, to be self-controlled and pure, to be busy at home, to be kind, and to be subject to their husbands, so that no one will malign the word of God. Titus 2:4-5

God asks a young woman to be busy at home and to love her family.

God asks older women to share their successes and experience.

A woman's life has seasons but in each season she is called to serve others.

To serve is to put the needs of others first. This includes serving meals, childcare, and homemaking. Many women abdicate homemaking tasks, such as providing meals, yet studies continue to show the most common factor among good students is eating meals as a family.

Being a homemaker is a career of dignity and fulfillment. For some women it is the sole career, for others it is the first career. A woman builds relationship, tradition, and memories for her family through homemaking. Years later a familiar scent or object may evoke a loving memory and connect the generations.

She is clothed with strength and dignity; she can laugh at the days to come. Proverbs 31:25

SPECIALIST	SERVICE OF A SERVANT	EXPRESSION OF LOVE
Nutritionist	Planning meals nutritional fitness.	I care about your health
Chef	Cooking	I give my time to care for you.
Home manager	Cleans, delegates chores, oversees repair workers	I believe order brings peace.
Fashion coordinator	Buying, making clothes	I want you to look good and be protected from the weather.
Wardrobe mistress	Washing clothes	I want you to look good. I care about keeping you germ free.
Interior designer	Decorating the home	I want to bring beauty to your life. I'm creating a place of refuge.
Financial planner	Spending money wisely	I care about your needs.
Investor	Saving, earning money	I care about your future.
Personal fitness manager	Exercising Encouraging children to exercise	I want to be healthy so I will be here for you. I want you to be healthy.
Good Samaritan	Serving the poor	I want to share God's love because he has blessed us.
Family network supporter	Praises her family	I want to express love to you.
Morale booster	Hugs her family members	I want to show love to you.
Spiritual discipler	Involved in Bible study	I want to be a godly woman.
Future planner	Develops hobbies/career	I want to grow as a person so the family can grow.
Social director	Commits time to family Plans social activities	I want to be available and plan fun times for us.
Time manager	Limits outside commitments	You are important.

Connecting a child's learning style to Jesus

Your hands made me and formed me; give me understanding to learn your commands. Psalm 119:73

Each child develops a learning style in which one approach of thinking dominates. Discover and use your child's learning style to connect your child to Jesus. These are six basic learning styles.

Visual learners (learn by sight) will enjoy a Bible with lots of pictures, maps, charts, and diagrams. They will also enjoy using reference books, memory cards, and computer based Bible games. Supply crayons and Bible coloring books to add color to stories.

Auditory (learn by listening) learners love to listen to someone reading the Bible stories. Try an audio Bible or audio Internet sites. They will also enjoy talking about the Bible story as a family and making their own tapes about God. As they grow they will want to debate and discuss Bible passages. Spend extra time praying aloud together.

Kinesthetic (learn while moving whole body, never sit still) learners thrive on multi-tasking of movement while listening to taped stories and videos. This learner may add to recall through using interactive web sites, Bible games that involve movement, drama groups, making Bible crafts, and songs with movements. Talk about the Bible while taking walks.

Tactile learners (like to touch and uses senses to learn) like object lessons and touching objects associated with Bible stories. They may listen better by candlelight. Coloring books, hands on activities, trying Bible foods, board games, making models, drawing, writing and journaling help Bible lessons sink in.

Global (social and spontaneous) learners like to study Bible people. They enjoy personal experiences stories and videos of modern day children that exemplify Bible truths. Use maps to talk about Bible places. Choral readings and group activities interest them.

Analytical (reasons and questions information, collects and organizes facts) learners enjoy a child's Bible with lots of reference material in it. They enjoy discussions and books that answer questions children ask about Jesus. Be patient and prepared as they ask lots of questions.

MORE IDEAS

- Encourage **kinesthetic** learners to make up motions for Bible songs.
- Have **tactile** learners dance to Bible songs and dramatize Bible passages.
- Let **auditory** learners retell stories with puppets.
- Encourage **analytical** children to search the Bible for answers to their questions.
- Let **visual** learners illustrate Bible stories.
- Help **tactile** and **global** children reach out to the community. Make sandwiches for the homeless, help neighbors, and invite friends to church.
- Create a backyard Bible carnival for the neighborhood that involves **all** learning styles.

Connecting a child's interests to Jesus

Train a child in the way he should go, and when he is old he will not turn from it. Proverbs 22:6

The Lord created each person with special talents. Connect Christ to a child's natural interest so they will see that Jesus is relevant to their own lives.

Art. Enjoy the artwork of sunsets and rainbows the Lord paints in the sky. Look at descriptions in the Bible as word paintings, especially the Psalms. Only people can be creative. Start a scrapbook of drawings of Bible stories. Have fun making things.

Cooking and celebrations. Try making foods Jesus would have eaten. Taste dates, nuts, figs, and flat, round, wheat bread. Celebrate a Seder meal to remember the Last Supper (Mark 14:22-25). Enjoy a picnic at the beach as Jesus did with his disciples (*John 21:1-14*). Read about Bible feasts and celebrations (Exodus 12:24-27; Leviticus 23; Esther 9:28-32). Invite Jesus to parties and set a special place for him.

Friendships. Study Bible friends such as David and Jonathan, Ruth and Naomi, Dorcas and her friends, and Jesus and his disciples. They had problems, conflicts, and good times together. Read and discuss the disagreement between Paul and Barnabas (*Acts 15:36-39*) and how a friend denied Jesus (*Matthew 26:69-75*).

Music. Listen to the Psalms, sing verses, read about singing and musical instruments in the Bible. Even Jesus enjoyed a hymn with friends (*Matthew* 26:30). Read Psalm 150, then make joyful noises to praise God and create your own songs. Listen to Christian music and song videos.

Nature. Read about animals and creation in the Bible (*Genesis* 1:24-25). Talk about how God did not make any two things the same. Discover how many different flowers and leaves you can find near your home. Buy and read devotions about animals. Go stargazing, take nature walks, and stop to thank Jesus for all creation.

Science. Do experiments with biblical analogies, such as yeast (mix a cup of flour, 1/2 cup of water, and yeast then watch it bubble as it rises). Investigate Scriptures that point to the multitude and differences of stars (*1 Corinthians* 15:41), and dinosaurs in Job 40. Investigate science and the Bible on the Internet (www.clarifyingchristianity.com/science.shtml and www.77talks.co.uk).

Sports. Compare the Holy Spirit with a coach. Discuss how discipline and training improve a person's natural ability. Relate how discipline in Bible study also improves attitudes and skills. Use Paul's comparison of an athlete's training in 1 Corinthians 9:24-27.

Connecting a child's personality to Jesus

For you created my inmost being; you knit me together in my mother's womb. Psalm 139:13

A child's personality gives clues for spiritual training methods. Gary Smalley depicted personalities with animals though there are other terms used.

Playful otter (Popular/sanguine) This optimistic child loves to make friends, play, and talk.

NURTURE STRENGTHS
- Teach about a personal relationship with Jesus.
- Keep devotions fun with variety.
- Look for Bible fun (Esther's beauty contest, Peter fished).
- Buy a Bible with pictures and activities.
- Find fun church programs for them.

HELP THEM OVERCOME WEAKNESSES
- Encourage setting and follow goals.
- Encourage thinking before speaking.

Lion (Powerful/choleric) This natural born leader sets goals and likes directing activities.

NURTURE STRENGTHS
- Explain God's purpose and plan for salvation.
- Read Bible of leaders (Paul, David, Deborah).
- Let them choose devotion materials.
- Let them lead devotions.
- Buy a Bible and matching journal.

HELP THEM OVERCOME WEAKNESSES
- Promote consideration of others.
- Let children see leader's problems. (Moses, Paul)

Beaver (Perfect/melancholy) This organized child completes tasks, but may be pessimistic.

NURTURE STRENGTHS
- Teach God's truths and sense of justice and right.
- Be consistent with time and devotions.
- Teach Bible stories that show failure (Eden, flood).
- Explore truths of salvation and Jesus.
- Help child choose a study Bible.
- Encourage your child to journal.

HELP THEM OVERCOME WEAKNESSES
- Encourage child to not be judgmental.
- Promote forgiveness.

Golden retriever (Peacemaker/phlegmatic) This peacemaker tells jokes and helps others relax.

NURTURE STRENGTHS
- Teach God's love and forgiveness.
- Share your relationship with Jesus
- Dwell on stories of compassion (Jesus healing, Joseph's family reunion).
- Use John 3:16 to show that Jesus' saving love.
- Use a concordance to find verses on peace.

HELP THEM OVERCOME WEAKNESSES
- Encourage completing tasks on time.
- Help child pray for what they cannot solve.

RESOURCES:

The Treasure Tree: Helping Kids Understand Their Personality by J.Trent, ISBN 0849958490

Personality Plus by F. Littauer, ISBN 0800744071

Nurturing spiritual growth of little ones

Jesus said, "Let the little children come to me, and do not hinder them, for the kingdom of heaven belongs to such as these."
Matthew 19:14

From pregnancy through the first two years, play Christian music and gently speak about Jesus to your baby. Pray aloud as you lay your little one in bed. As the toddler years begin and language develops share simple messages of God's love and bring Jesus into your activities.

BRING CHRIST INTO PLAY

Play games babies like, such as peek-a-boo or hide and seek. At times say "God sees you." Ask if they hid in a fluffy cloud, inside a tree trunk, in a hole with a worm, or other silly place, who could still find them?

DANCE AND SING TO CELEBRATE AND PRAISE THE LORD TOGETHER

- Play and dance to children's Christian music.
- Sing the words together.
- Talk about what the words tell them about Jesus.
- Blow kisses to Jesus during and after singing.

CAPTURE MEMORIES

- Take photos of your child's first time at church, first religious events, and of you praying for your child.
- Make a spiritual scrapbook. Write in your child's first prayer, favorite Christian storybook, and other special moments.

℘

MAKE SIMPLE CONNECTIONS

- Use what a child knows to talk about what Jesus would do.
- Jesus sees everything. Let him catch us being good, not bad.
- As you can wash dirt off hands, so Jesus washes away sin.
- A bandage can cover an outside hurt and help it heal. Christ's love can heal the inside hurt in the heart.
- Help your child learn to say, "I'm sorry" and pray with them for Jesus to forgive their sins.

℘

ABCs OF SALVATION

As children start pre-reading skills and learn the alphabet, introduce salvation ABCs:

Admit that you sin and need Jesus to forgive you. *(Romans 3:23)*

Believe Jesus died to save you. *(John 3:16 and 1 John 4:10b)*

Call on God to make you his child. *(Romans 10:13)*

Nurturing spiritual growth of elementary aged children

And the boy Samuel continued to grow in stature and in favor with the LORD and with men. 1 Samuel 2:26

At this age children are curious and developing many skills. They are also ready to grow spiritually..

BIBLE STORIES

Connect problems of Bible people to everyday problems. Read and talk about Bible people and events, such as connecting Cain and Abel with sibling rivalry and anger management. Look for books that combine the stories with learning, such as *Let's Chat About the Bible* (Barbour Publishing).

PRAYER

Help children pray aloud. Discuss prayer requests and answers. Record them in a prayer journal or on slips or paper in a blessing's jar. Read prayer answers at celebrations and times child feels discouraged.

Read Bible prayers as models. *(Exodus 15:1-18; Psalm 23; Nehemiah 1:6-11, 2:4, and Luke 11:2-4.)*

DISCOVERING GOD TOGETHER

Study Bible families. *(Noah, Genesis 8-9; Ruth, Book of Ruth; Joseph, Genesis 37, 42-46; Lazarus, John 11-12:11; and Paul and Aquila in Acts 18:1-3, 24-28.)*

DEVELOP TALENTS

Praise talents as gifts from God. Discuss that God has a plan for everyone's life and will use those talents. Finding these gifts is a lifelong treasure hunt! No one is good at everything and that's okay.

Encourage children to develop talents. Match gifts with activities or lessons, such as music lessons for the musically talented child, sport teams for the natural athlete, or opportunities to visit nursing homes of children who show great compassion.

PRAISE BIBLICAL VIRTUES

Show appreciation when a child exhibits any virtue (Mercy, kindness, joy). Affirmation reinforces good behavior.

HOOK INTO CHURCH PROGRAMS

Help children find others who love the Lord in Sunday school, children's church, church clubs, and other programs that nourish spiritual growth. These programs compliment home teachings. Volunteer in these areas. Reinforce lessons taught.

LET THEM QUESTION FAITH

Don't fear questions. If stumped, check the Bible. Let them bring tough questions to church.

CAPTURE MEMORIES

- Encourage your child to journal.
- Take photos of special events at church.
- Record questions asked and answers that satisfied.
- Record some of your child's prayers.
- Photograph and write about family devotions.

Nurturing spiritual growth of tweens

But grow in the grace and knowledge of our Lord and Savior Jesus Christ. To him be glory both now and forever! Amen.
2 Peter 3:18

As tweens start puberty they begin struggling for independence, often through rebellious behavior. Encourage growth but set boundaries. Peer groups become more influential so get to know your child's friends. Help tweens incorporate godly values into morality and decision-making.

KEYS TO SPIRITUAL GROWTH

- Encourage personal devotions, Bible reading, and prayer. Reinforce success with privileges or rewards.

- Tweens are often self-critical. Remind them that God loves them and has plans for them. Find devotional books with humor. It will help them learn to laugh at mistakes.

- Let your tween lead family devotions and choose family activities. Attend some Christian concerts together.

- Connect biblical behavior and consequences for bad choices. Read about the kings and consequences of turning away from God.

- Raise your child for responsibility. With daughters look at the *Proverbs 31* woman and see what skills she ought to develop. Let sons study the disciples and King David to explore areas to develop or avoid.

❀ Explain that rights and privileges come with showing responsibility and good choices. As they seek independence discuss what responsibilities are required. Talk about *Luke 12:48b*.

❀ Try showing your child various ways to study Scripture. (Verse, topical, character studies, etc.).

❀ Set age-appropriate boundaries, including church attendance. If your tween lives at home and you choose that your household will follow the Lord then they need to go to church with you.

ß

CAPTURE THE MEMORIES

❀ Record your tween's spiritual growth.

❀ Photograph your tween studying the Bible and attending youth group functions.

❀ Note your child's spiritual gifts and record how they are being used and developed.

Nurturing spiritual growth of older children

When I was a child, I talked like a child, I thought like a child, I reasoned like a child. When I became a man, I put childish ways behind me. 1 Corinthians 13:11

As teens transition to adulthood they make life choices. That's scary for everyone! The most important task parents tackle is keeping communication lines open.

KEYS TO SPIRITUAL GROWTH

- Equip your child with Bible reference materials such as a concordance, biographies of Christian heroes, Bible atlas, cyclopedic index, etc.
- Support your teen's good choices. Pray through the bad ones but be open to forgiving and helping a prodigal change.
- Affirm your child even if you disagree with choices. Let them know you believe in God's plans for them and that they make the sound, godly choices.
- Recruit your son or daughter to join a ministry to work together (i.e. class aid).
- Let older children teach younger siblings.
- Suggest that your budding young adult take a summer mission trip.
- Appreciate your young adult. Express thanks for helping, driving, running errands, and doing well,

even for beautiful smiles.
Compliment good attitudes, too.

- ❧ Share in their joys and sorrows.
  Don't pass out platitudes. Listen and
  feel the joy or disappointment with
  them. Share your experiences.

- ❧ Accept your child's strong points
  and limitations. Guide them in
  matching strong points and passions
  to career decisions.

- ❧ Keep expressing love even when
  they act like they don't want it.

- ❧ Pick your battles and don't worry
  over trivial differences.

- ❧ Be open to dating/courting partners.
  The person could become part of
  the family!

- ❧ Keep communicating. Email your college/service
  child who is away. They may get busy and not
  reply, but they will read the emails. If you express
  humor and love they are more likely to respond.
  If you continue to let them know you are praying
  for them and are always available they will
  appreciate it. Add a 1-800-line to be affordably
  reachable or get children cell phones/beepers.

ɞ

CAPTURE THE MEMORIES

- ❧ Keep emails and letters sent from summer camps,
  mission trips, and college.

- ❧ Photograph important times, such as getting a
  driver's license and that first time driving alone!

- ❧ Pray together before each momentous occasion.

Godly discipline

Discipline *your son, and he will give you peace; he will bring delight to your soul. Proverbs 29:17*

Discipline has two meanings.

TRAINING

Discipline is "training" and "instruction" that develops character and talent. It requires practice. Help children become self-disciplined.

TRAINING TIPS

- Establish and follow routines, such as brushing teeth in the morning and evening.
- Regular Bible study develops spiritual character.
- Create study areas and schedule for schoolwork/homework (at a set).
- Reinforce good habits (stickers for tots, extra playtime for young children, phone or TV/computer time for older children).
- Discuss how training helps people mature. Read and discuss 1 Corinthians 9:25 and Ephesians 6:4.
- Allow some control. You may set the time of day for a chore, but let child choose the specific starting time.
- Encourage stewardship. Let them choose where to give their tithe or ways to raise money to give.
- Follow through on commitments (practice music lessons, timely arrival for sport events).

CORRECTION

Discipline's other meaning is "correction" It eliminates
bad habits and develops good behavior. Correction
is not abusive. A shepherd used a rod to guide and
protect sheep, not to beat them.

> Partner with your spouse to correct children.
> Be consistent (same problem/same consequence).
> Set appropriate consequences for infractions.

No **discipline** *seems pleasant at the time, but painful. Later
on, however, it produces a harvest of righteousness and peace for
those who have been trained by it. Hebrews* 12:11

CORRECTION TIPS
- Don't correct or argue while angry. Cool down first.
- Use tough love and seek professional help if
  needed. (Drugs and addictions)
- Set rules. When new situations arise pray and set
  a new rule. Be specific. Show how to follow each
  rule and explain its importance
- Establish appropriate consequences. Examples:
  No playtime if room is left messy. Use time to clean.
  After hurting a sibling, serve that person or do
  his chores.
- Model good behavior.
- Be consistent. Stick to rules.
- Follow through quickly with consequences.
- Praise and encourage correct behavior.
- Pray and express love after discipline is carried out.

SAMPLE CONSEQUENCES (for cheating)
- Confession.
- Pray together for forgiveness.
- Explain disappointment and trust issues.
- Extra project assigned as restitution.

Christ in conflicts

What causes fights and quarrels among you? Don't they come from your desires that battle within you? James 4:1

JESUS RESPONDED TO CONFLICTS

- ❀ He pointed out a brother's greed. *(Luke 12:13-15)*
- ❀ He used Scripture against Satan's taunts. *(Luke 4:1-12)*
- ❀ He answered deceitful questions with truth and calm debate. *(Matthew 22:15-40)*.
- ❀ He forgave those who hurt him. *(Luke 23:34)*

MODEL AND TEACH ANGER MANAGEMENT SKILLS:

- ❀ Release anger in acceptable way (running, shaking your body, dancing, stomping feet, or drawing).
- ❀ Understand consequences of expressing anger in a hurtful way that breaks rules.
- ❀ Delay confrontation until calm.
- ❀ Identify the real cause/problem.
- ❀ Pray and consider how Jesus would react.
- ❀ Use "I" statements ("I feel hurt when anyone hits me.").
- ❀ Try to understand the other side of the problem.
- ❀ Take ten slow breaths.
- ❀ Talk about your feelings and the situation.
- ❀ Relax with music or thinking of something funny.
- ❀ Switch to a more comfortable activity.

SEEK PROFESSIONAL HELP IN THE EVENT OF

Rage

Abuse (physical or emotional)

Endangerment

Unresolved conflicts with major relational problems

Addictions

ℬ

12 STEPS TO RESOLVING CONFLICTS

1. Meet in a neutral place when everyone is calm.

2. Identify and define the problem. Stick to the issue.

3. List each person's desires, needs, and reasons for his/her position. Consider if any are selfish or impractical. Ask questions to understand choices. Don't attack one another. Avoid "always" and "never" statements.

4. Brainstorm possible solutions.

5. Be flexible.

6. List possible compromises.

7. List pros and cons of each proposed solution and how each person benefits.

8. Pray together and forgive one another.

9. Choose one solution. Look for one where all benefit in some way. Agree to try it wholeheartedly.

10. Set a time to evaluate the solution.

11. Implement the plan.

12. Evaluate outcome at set date.

ℬ

Christ in hard times

For just as the sufferings of Christ flow over into our lives, so also through Christ our comfort overflows. 2 Corinthians 1:5

Hard times come to almost every family. It may be divorce, death, loss, moving, natural disaster, illness, financial setbacks, strained or broken relationships, a prodigal situation, or other problems.

BAD THINGS CAN HAPPEN BECAUSE

- ❁ God allows choice. Evil choices cause pain.
- ❁ Natural disasters, accidents, and illnesses are consequences of living in a fallen world. These problems strengthen us, help us grow, and remind us of life in heaven without tears. (*James 1:2-4, Revelation 7:17*)
- ❁ Faith is tested, as with Job and Peter. (*Job 1:6-11, Luke 22:31-32*)
- ❁ They bring God glory as with a blind man Jesus healed. (*John 9:1-3*)
- ❁ Persecution helps spread the kingdom of God. (*Acts 21:13-14*)

IT TAKES TIME TO RECOVER AS YOU

Take in the reality and truth of circumstances.
Identify and cope with grief.
Make adjustments to new situations.
Experience new hope and new joy.

COPING DURING HARD TIMES

Ruth lost all, through death and famine, except a broken mother-in-law and faith. She labored for food.

Through the daily process of trusting, God healed two hearts and brought new joy. Her hope is seen in Ruth 1:16, "Your people will be my people and your God my God." God blessed her with a new family and she became an ancestor of Christ.

TIPS FOR COPING

- Continually pray for God's help.
- Take life one day at a time. If pain seems unbearable, take one hour or one minute at a time.
- Understand stages of grief can come in any order: shock, denial, anger, bargaining, depression, acceptance, adjustment, hope.
- Adjust your life slowly. Most people handle big challenges but stumble over the small ones.
- Exercise to raise endorphin levels and reduce stress.
- Do a forgiveness inventory. Forgive people who hurt you.
- Forgive yourself for mistakes and poor judgment.
- Dwell on blessings and Jesus' sacrifice for you.
- Cry. Tears are cathartic and promote healing.
- Give yourself small tasks each day and do them.
- Listen to uplifting music. Sing praises or hymns.
- Help another hurting person. It lessens self-pity.
- Seek professional help for deep depression.
- Express love to others who are suffering.
- Talk to friends, pastor, or counselors.
- Tell God how you really feel.
- Join a support group.
- Let others comfort you.
- Read Psalms, Job, and Ruth.
- Confess any sin and release guilt.
- Journal.
- Get plenty of rest.

Forgiveness and restitution

Be kind and compassionate to one another, forgiving each other, just as in Christ God forgave you. Ephesians 4:32

In living together we experience many instances of hurting one another and feeling hurt. Forgiveness helps a family live in harmony.

FORGIVE OTHERS

Christ asks us to follow his example and forgive others, as he did while on the cross (*Luke 23:34*), even if they are not sorry.

STEPS IN RECONCILIATION IN THE HOME

1. The offender needs to understand and admit they hurt someone. When unaware of hurting someone, he or she may need to have the problem explained. For example, "When you dashed outside you slammed the door on my foot."
2. The offender needs to confess/apologize to God and the person hurt. (The prodigal son's return to his father gives us an example, Luke 15:21.)
3. To really repent the person should consider how to avoid repeating the offense. For example, the door slammer could decide to look before closing doors.
4. Within the family, the offended person needs to forgive to restore the relationship.

5. Add an exchange of affection such as a hug, handshake, or compliment.

"In your anger do not sin": Do not let the sun go down while you are still angry. Ephesians 4:26

RESTITUTION AND RESTORATION

Set a family rule that after forgiveness you take action. Do a kind deed for the person hurt. This promotes restoration.

- ❀ If a child hurts another physically let that child make restitution through service. For example, if a boy hits his brother's leg, let him be the leg for the other by getting things for them, doing their chores, etc.
- ❀ If you break something, try to fix it or give the person something of your own.
- ❀ Ask what will help the hurt person feel better and try to do it.
- ❀ When a child disobeys a parent they must also accept any punishment or consequence already set up in the family rules.

℘

Zaccheus changed when he met Jesus. He had cheated people in the past. He chose to make restitution, that is, to make up for the hurt. He decided to give back four times anything he had taken through cheating (*Luke 19:8*). For Zaccheus, forgiving = 4 giving, that is giving 4 times back.

Character development

but we were gentle among you, like a mother caring for her little children… For you know that we dealt with each of you as a father deals with his own children, encouraging, comforting and urging you to live lives worthy of God, who calls you into his kingdom and glory. 1 Thessalonians 2:7b,11-12

WHAT DOES IT MEAN TO NURTURE?

To nurture means to cultivate. A gardener tends a beautiful plant by watering, exposing it to sunlight, and protecting it from weeds, disease, and pestilence.

Families nurture character through conversation, praise, modeling virtues, and by providing experiences that encourage character. Consider what character traits you want each person to develop. Set them as goals.

TEN GODLY CHARACTER TRAITS (add more you want to encourage) Each produces other positive traits.

Compassion leads to kindness and generosity.

Contentment guards against jealousy and envy.

Faithfulness leads to spiritual growth and holiness.

Honesty builds integrity.

Justice moves hearts to mercy.

Love promotes patience and understanding.

Loyalty builds unity and promotes caring for other's needs.

Perseverance helps a person succeed and overcome obstacles.

Responsibility leads to maturity, good work ethic, and self-respect.

Respect for authority brings order and harmony.

TIPS TO ENCOURAGE CHARACTER

Communicate. Conversations build relationship and transmit values.

Help others. Putting others first encourages compassion.

Always pray for each person's character growth.

Read about heroes with character.

Applaud each person's good virtues.

Commit to modeling virtues yourself.

Tell stories of family members of character.

Enjoy family traditions. Rituals identify and celebrate values.

Recognize and capture teachable moments.

℘

FAILURE AS OPPORTUNITY

Failure reminds us we still need to grow. A child can choose to work to improve. Through practice and numerous falls a child learns to ride a bicycle and develops perseverance. Talk and discover lessons after a failure, Brainstorm about future attempts or decisions, and any need for assistance to learn.

GROWTH THROUGH TRIALS

Provide comfort and support when a family member faces a trial, whether it is school or job related, broken friendship, or a hardship. Actively listen. Only give advice if asked or if safety is a concern. Pray and trust that God will use the trial to nurture character.

Sharing Christ

He said to them, "Go into all the world and preach the good news to all creation." Mark 16:15

Love of Christ in a family should spill over into the lives of others as a waterfall that spills over a dam of an overflowing lake. Small trickles of kindness, concern, and compassion will run off in all directions.

Be sure your children understand their faith and can share it with others. Let them memorize *John 3:16* and use it to help tell others that Jesus died to save them. Encourage family members to share answers to prayer at home and to give a testimony of how God has worked in their lives.

In the same way, let your light shine before men, that they may see your good deeds and praise your Father in heaven. Matthew 5:16

Choose to reach out and serve so others may see God's love in action.

WAYS TO SERVE OTHERS

- Give used toys, books, and clothes to the poor.
- Help make sandwiches for the homeless. Help transport the food to a shelter.
- Invite singles to your home for a meal or family evening of games.
- If someone is ill tell them you will pray for them and do that as a family.
- Make extra cookies, when baking, and give them to a neighbor or shut-in.
- Visit elderly at nursing homes. Offer to make and donate tray favors.
- Take part in a church ministry that helps needy people.
- Volunteer to watch children for a single mom.
- Remember to pray when dining out.
- Take your children shopping before Christmas and buy toys for the poor.
- Buy and give maternity clothes and baby items to a pregnancy center.
- Take part in walkathons for important causes, such as right to life.
- Choose to support a mission or a child. Decide to give up dessert weekly or other sacrifice to provide support money.
- Let your children help choose where to donate your charity money.
- Invite your children's friends to join in family devotions.

Home as a haven

By wisdom a house is built, and through understanding it is established; through knowledge its rooms are filled with rare and beautiful treasures. Proverbs 24:3-4

Home should offer a retreat from the world where each person feels comfortable, finds rest, shelter, and acceptance. Each room should fill a family member with treasured memories, joy, and hope.

MAKE YOUR HOME COMFORTABLE

Have a room with comfortable seats where people can relax, talk or play games.

Stock healthy snacks to refresh family members.

Encourage others to lovingly accept each person's uniqueness. Model it yourself.

Don't compare children or place unrealistic expectations on anyone.

Let your children know when they can invite friends over.

Teach everyone to be hospitable to company.

Smile when you look at your loved ones.

FILL THE HOME WITH BEAUTY AND ORDER

Keep the home clean and organized. Enlist family support to do this.

Add touches of beauty and color.

Keep a living room ready for guests.

Resource: www.messies.com.

CREATE A SAFE SHELTER FROM THE WORLD

> Monitor electrical outlets, cords, and appliances for safety.
>
> If young ones are in the home, make it a safe environment (Cover electrical outlets. Lockup poisonous cleaners and breakables, etc,)
>
> Use appropriate locks and security systems for your neighborhopod.
>
> Keep communication open and friendly. Listen more and talk less.
>
> Be open so children will feel at ease talking about difficult problems (i.e. bullying or abuse).
>
> Obtain and check references for babysitters.
>
> Hold meetings to discuss improvements.

CREATE MEMORIES

> Let favorite recipes become traditional meals.
>
> Take photos and place them in scrapbooks.
>
> Schedule family times and include fun activities.
>
> Incorporate your heritage or traditions at holidays.
>
> Create your own family traditions.

BUILD COMMUNICATION SKILLS AT ALL TIMES

> ✿ Speak with love.
>
> ✿ Smile when speaking. Love will be in your voice.
>
> ✿ Talk about a problem while it is still small.
>
> ✿ Note how often you speak, your tone and words.
>
> ✿ Speak random words of kindness and praise to sprinkle your children with joy.
>
> ✿ Listen. Ask questions to be sure you understand.
>
> ✿ Give clear, specific directions. Ask the listener to repeat the message.
>
> ✿ Consider the words someone speaks you as a gift.

The Lord guard your going out

*He [the Lord] guards you when you leave and when
you return, he guards you now, he guards you always.*
Psalm 121:8 (MSG)

As children venture into the world they enter places
   and meet people who do not hold Christian views
   or share your family values.
   It is vital to pray with and for your children
   upon their going out.

GUARD THE GOING OUT

❀ Know where each person is going and with whom.

❀ Let your family know how to reach you.

❀ Get to know parents of your children's friends.

❀ Get to know coaches and teachers in authority
   over your children.

❀ Check movies to know what you and your
   children choose to watch.

❀ www.entertainment.planetwisdom.com and
   www.pluggedinonline.com review movies from
   Christian perspective and give discussion questions
   for families.

❀ Once a child can drive, decide when they can
   transport family members or friends.

❀ Do not leave or let others leave home angry.
   Stop and settle problems first.

❁ Watch the clothing your child chooses.
Discuss what messages clothes can send out to
others. Set dress codes. Be sure your clothes are
also well chosen.

❁ Guard how much fast food is being consumed.
Discuss nutrition and good choices for eating out
as well as limiting how often the family dines
out or orders fast food.

❁ List free activities outside the home, such as
nature walks, bicycling, playing in a park, going
to the library, and attending church events.

❁ Guard the tongue. Discuss honoring and
respecting family members and what subjects
should not be shared outside the home.

B

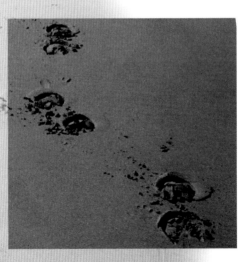

...and coming in

Above all else, guard your heart, for it is the wellspring of life.
Proverbs 4:23

Guard what is brought into the home as that guards
hearts. Limit electronic entertainment. You may
want to let your children earn extra time by letting
one minute of reading or sports = one minute of
entertainment. The incentive promotes reading and
physical activity.

TELEVISION

Process television viewing, including commercials.
Watch shows together and discuss values. Ask,
"What would Jesus do?" to decide if the show
is permissible in the home.

Check Christian web sites that review shows
(www.gospelcom.net/preview). Some even have
discussion questions.

Buy something advertised and test it to see if it lives
up to the ad. That can teach discernment and help
children see that commercials often exaggerate.

BOOKS

Reviews for many books can be found at online
bookstores. If a child desires to read a questionable
book, agree to read it and discuss it together. Also
agree to discard the book if it is unacceptable.

VIDEO GAMES

Check game ratings and set a bar for what rating
is okay to play. Check reviews online at
www.gradingthemovies.com/html/games.shtml and
www.plaingames.com
Play video games with your children.

MUSIC

Listen to song lyrics and investigate the artists. You can
often find the words on the Internet.

CCM magazine and *Plugged In* magazines provide reviews
of music groups. Also www.planetwisdom reviews
top artists, bands, and songs.

FRIENDS AND THEIR LANGUAGE

Let your children's friends know swearing and cursing
are off limits. Give gentle reminders as needed.

Pass out a breath mint as children enter as a reminder
that 'a clean mouth' means clean language!

INTERNET

Your web provider may include a
pornography blocker. Otherwise buy
one. Turn on any filtering available.

Discuss Internet responsibility and how
anyone can post urban legends and
propaganda.

Help find reliable sites for school research.

Consider filtering email. Or have all email
sent to you and forward acceptable ones

GOSSIP

Discuss how to curb gossip. Practice it. Discuss
scary rumors, but don't dwell on them.
Investigate possible problems, but guard against gossip.

Proverbs 31
woman

Charm is deceptive, and beauty is fleeting; but a woman who fears the LORD is to be praised. Proverbs 31:30

This is an ideal woman of faith who fears the Lord.
Proverbs reveals that the fear of the Lord is the
beginning of wisdom (1:7); a fountain of life (14:27);
and causes a person to hate evil (8:13).

Proverbs 31:10-31 describes a mature woman who has
developed talents and virtues over time.
She has a relationship with the Lord. The whole
family benefits because she is relaxed, organized,
and in control. Her standards reveal godly goals
for women in seven key areas.

SEVEN AREAS FOR WOMEN OF FAITH
TO DEVELOP
- Supportive wife
  Respects her husband
  Trustworthy
  Marriage is a partnership
  She is her husband's companion
    or friend
  She is loved and honored
- Loving mother/devoted to family
  Nourishes family with good food
  Good listener
  Clothes her family

Family lives in peace
Respectful children who praise her
❀ Disciplined, diligent woman
Physically fit
Faithful steward of time
Well dressed
Woman of dignity
Manages household well
Develops her talents
Manages workers well (modern women make
   good use of appliances)
❀ Financially wise
A bargain hunter
Investigates before investing
Saves money
Sets a budget and sticks to it
Budget includes beautiful clothes
Entrepreneur
Turn hobbies into money earning opportunities
Develops a career that blends with family
Contributes to family income
❀ Minister to the poor
Find ways to help the poor
Takes part in ministry to the poor
Gives to the poor (on tight budgets, be creative
   and hold a yard sale to raise funds or participate
   in charity walks)
❀ Discreet and wise with words
Not a gossip
Shares experience with kindness
Does not put down family members or others
Mentors others

Peace in the home

My people will live in peaceful dwelling places, in secure homes, in undisturbed places of rest. Isaiah 32:18

PEACE comes from harmonizing unique differences. (This does not mean accepting sinful behavior).

> **P**raise each person's positive actions and talents.
> **E**agerly open your ears and listen to one another.
> **A**ccept individuals as God made them.
> **C**onsider other's needs before your own.
> **E**ntreat God in prayer.

SIBLINGS

Siblings often compete for parental attention. If one perceives another receives more or better quality attention, jealousy can fester.

- Daily give each child undivided attention.
- Avoid comparisons.
- Praise each child's talents, efforts, and successes.
- Set consequences for sibling squabbles.
- Help siblings learn to forgive one another.

GIVE AWAY WORRIES

- Dwell on your blessings.
- Maintain a positive attitude and trust in God.
- Ask others to pray for you.
- Do your best, with all your heart.
- Work on problems one-step at a time.